FINAL REPORT

FAIR MARKET VALUE ANALYSIS
FOR A FIBER OPTIC CABLE PERMIT
IN
NATIONAL MARINE SANCTUARIES

August 2002

NATIONAL OCEANIC AND ATMOSPHERIC ADMINISTRATION
NATIONAL OCEAN SERVICE
NATIONAL MARINE SANCTUARY PROGRAM

TABLE OF CONTENTS

I. INTRODUCTION

The National Marine Sanctuary Program (NMSP) evaluates special-use permit applications by companies seeking to place and maintain fiber optic cables in National Marine Sanctuaries. The National Marine Sanctuaries Act allows the NMSP to issue a special-use permit for the presence of cables on the sanctuary floor and, if an application is approved, NMSP may collect certain administrative and monitoring fees. In addition, NMSP is entitled to receive fair market value for the permitted use of sanctuary resources.

This document develops an approach to assessing fair market value for the presence of a submarine fiber-optic cable in a National Marine Sanctuary. It is based on dozens of industry and government sources and draws on the collaboration and review of numerous experts in business, legal and technical arenas. A final determination of fair market value should include consideration of current market conditions and any available recent data, in addition to the analysis contained in this report.

The research and analysis is organized as follows: Part Two presents an overview of the marine sanctuary system, the fiber-optics industry, and the permitting process. Part Three describes the major approaches to valuing a right of way, the private-market analogue to granting sanctuary access. Part Four describes the protection of sanctuary resources and the importance of accommodating the telecommunications infrastructure. Part Five summarizes permitting activities at other government agencies. Part Six presents the analysis of fair market value for a sanctuary permit based on the relevant valuation methods. Part Seven presents recommendations and conclusions regarding the appropriate valuation approach.

II. BACKGROUND AND OVERVIEW

National Marine Sanctuaries

The National Marine Sanctuary Program was established in 1972, coinciding with the 100th anniversary of the founding of the first national park. The Program's mission is to designate areas of the marine environment that have special natural or cultural significance and manage and protect them for future generations. There are currently thirteen national marine sanctuaries encompassing ocean gardens, near-shore coral reefs, whale migration corridors, deep-sea canyons, and underwater archeological sites. They range in size from Fagatele Bay Sanctuary, covering one-quarter square mile in American Samoa, to Monterey Bay Sanctuary, one of the largest marine protected areas in the world, covering over 5,300 square miles along the coast of California. Total sanctuary territory encompasses just under 18,000 square miles, about the size of Vermont and New Hampshire combined.

The sanctuaries are monitored for water quality, the ecological impact of fishing, the accidental release of chemicals and other environmental concerns. Many lie adjacent to some of the country's most pristine coastlines, including protected coastal habitats and national parks. While some activities are regulated or prohibited, certain others are allowed or encouraged. For example, such economically significant uses as shipping and commercial fishing are generally allowed within sanctuaries, although these activities may be restricted to protect sanctuary resources. Recreation, research and educational activities are encouraged, along with outreach efforts to foster resource protection and conservation awareness.

Fiber Optics Industry Overview

Over the past two decades, the development and expansion of fiber-optic networks has transformed the telecommunications market. Through higher transmission capacity, decreased interruptions in service, greater security and improved cost efficiency, fiber optic telecommunications cables are meeting increased demand for high-quality telephone, Internet, and data-transmission services. In the United States, both land-based networks and undersea intercontinental connections have added thousands of miles of new routes over the past few years.

As this report is written, a recession in the United States and an economic slowdown worldwide has dampened demand for telecommunications services and fiber-optic cable deployment. Many companies in the fiber-optics industry, with its high levels of up-front investment keyed to expectations of rapid growth, have experienced difficult financial conditions. But the drop-off in demand and investment is expected to be temporary. Industry analysts project a deviation from the upward trend in fiber-optic cable deployment coinciding with the dip in the business cycle. Total investment in submarine cable networks from 1986 to 1998 was $17 billion, representing about 400,000 route kilometers.[1] Investment in undersea optical-cable networks rose from less than $2 billion annually in 1998 to $6 billion in 2000. Projections by KMI Corporation, a leading industry analyst, indicate that the rate of new cable deployment is expected to return to an upward trend in 2003 and exceed previous levels in 2004.[2] Undersea cables were a part of the analysis, and followed a similar trend.

As of the date of this report, three fiber optic cable projects have been allowed to transit marine sanctuaries. They are the "Hibernia Transatlantic Project" (with a connection from Boston to Ireland that crosses the Stellwagen Bank Sanctuary), "Pacific Crossing 1" (from Japan to Seattle crossing the Olympic Coast sanctuary) and "Alaska United" (from Alaska to Seattle crossing the Olympic Coast sanctuary). The Alaska United project was completed before NMSP had examined the issue of fiber-optic cables in sanctuaries. The permits for the Pacific Crossing 1 and Hibernia projects included language that required payment of fair market value for the use of sanctuary resources once the appropriate value is assessed.

The Permitting Process and Fair Market Value
The National Marine Sanctuaries Act (NMSA) allows the Secretary of Commerce to issue special-use permits authorizing the conduct of specific activities in National Marine Sanctuaries and establishing conditions of access and use for marine sanctuary resources.

The presence of a fiber-optic cable on the floor of a sanctuary is a use for which a permit may be issued. According to the NMSA, the Secretary may assess and collect a fee that includes the cost of issuing the permit, as well as monitoring and other costs incurred as a result of the permitted activity. In addition, the fee must include "an amount which represents the fair market value of the use of the sanctuary resource."

In addition to issuing a special-use permit, sanctuary authorities must review and authorize an Army Corps permit for any cable project that includes a sanctuary crossing. The permitting process of the Army Corps of Engineers covers installation, maintenance and removal of a cable throughout U.S. waters. Potential harm to the undersea environment from cable installation is examined in an environmental review under the National Environmental Policy Act. NMSP is developing a set of principles to guide the installation of cables in marine sanctuaries and is working to ensure that, when a cable project is allowed, environmental impacts will be minimal and appropriately mitigated. Those principles were published for comment in an advance notice of proposed rulemaking (65 FR 51264, Aug. 23, 2000). NOAA is currently reviewing comments received on this notice.

Installation, maintenance, and removal of the cables are subject to sanctuary oversight through the Army Corps permitting process. Because some amount of injury may to occur during cable installation, and because by law the special-use permit cannot apply to any activity causing injury, the specific special use being authorized by NMSP is the long-term presence of the cables on the sanctuary seabed.

In 1993 the Office of Management and Budget (OMB) issued its most recent directive concerning fair market value and fees charged for the use of Federal resources. OMB Circular No. A-25[3] requires federal agencies to assess a user charge against each identifiable recipient for a service or privilege that confers special benefits. As with the granting of a fiber-optic permit, such a privilege "enables the beneficiary to obtain more immediate or substantial gains or values (which may or may not be measurable in monetary terms) than those that accrue to the general public." A government service is also designated as a special benefit if it is "performed at the request of or for the convenience of the recipient." The directive further states, "user charges will be based on market prices."

Market prices involving the use of property for the presence of fiber-optic cables can be observed in the market for rights of way. Telecommunication companies typically do not own the land used for a fiber optic network. Rather, companies purchase easements from landholders allowing rights of access for cables and cable conduits across numerous properties. It is this system of right-of-way purchases that allows a cable network to be created.

The issue of "fair market value" or "market price" for cable access to sanctuaries is complicated by the presence of non-market amenities. The value of a marine sanctuary lies in the conservation of a marine environment deemed to have special significance. Many people receive pleasure in knowing that the sanctuaries exist and are protected. These individual values, added up over millions of people, may have tremendous value, but little economic information about the extent of this value is revealed in market transactions.

This report relies on a comparison between the granting of a sanctuary permit and the sale of a fiber-optic right of way on private land. Numerous private-market precedents exist for the appraisal and sale of such right-of-way easements. This report also considers the amenity value of a sanctuary, but for a number of reasons this value is not specifically estimated and is not part of the calculation of fair market value. It is believed that the analysis of market transactions alone results in a reasonable special-use fee based on sound and thorough economic and policy considerations.

III. VALUING RIGHTS OF WAY

As noted previously, right-of-way transactions are a close analogue to the issuance of a permit allowing a fiber optic cable to cross a marine sanctuary. This section explores the concept of fair market value in the appraisal of right-of-way easements, relying on precedents and practices from several sources. Private sector practitioners use a variety of rules and methodologies to assist in easement negotiations. Numerous judicial proceedings have examined the appropriate use of fair market value in compensation for eminent domain takings. There is also a considerable body of literature in appraisal and real estate journals that explores the available approaches to assessing right-of-way values.

There is currently some debate regarding which set of legal and market precedents are appropriate for fair market analysis of fiber optic easements. On federal land, the focus has traditionally been loss to the seller. The decline in the value of a property due to buried cables was considered to be relatively small, and valuations reflected that. In the private sector, the gain to the buyer has received greater emphasis in price negotiations. The substantial revenues generated by the fiber optic industry have recently resulted in rapidly increasing prices for fiber-optic rights of way.

In the sections that follow, guidance from the available sources is presented and four general approaches to valuation are described. First, a set of land-based appraisal methods is examined. This traditional appraisal approach relies on the value of adjacent land and an assessment of relevant damage to solve the valuation problem. Second, the concept of a willing buyer and seller is described. By examining the incentives of the parties involved, characteristics of a fair market outcome can be explored. Next, examples of income-based valuation are presented. These methods employ the notion that a communications right of way is a valuable part of a business enterprise and that a portion of enterprise income should be allocated to this right-of-way asset. Finally, the use of comparable market transactions is described. Past transactions are rarely an exact precedent, but they serve as a guide to price levels and overall market trends, and they incorporate elements of the other valuation methods.

Land-Based Appraisal

Appraisal techniques for right-of-way transactions frequently rely on the value of the occupied land. Such land-based or "fee-simple" values focus on the property rights bestowed by the seller. The basis of value is the "before and after rule," using the difference between two estimates of a parcel's value: before the easement is granted and after the new use is in place. Ownership of a property is thought to entail a "bundle of rights" for the owner. Some of these rights are sold off when an easement is granted, but those rights remaining still retain value. The before-and-after rule results in modest value estimates based on loss to the seller.

In applying the before-and-after rule, some benchmark value is needed for the land under consideration. The across-the-fence (ATF) rule holds that a given parcel is worth about the same as similar neighboring land. The ATF approach generates a "fee-simple" value for a parcel. That is, it ignores any special use of the land that might create additional value. A railroad right of way that crosses several states, for example, would be valued based on total land area. The fact that the land is composed of a continuous corridor rather than a collection of disjointed parcels would not affect the ATF estimate of value.

In contrast to these approaches, the notion of "corridor value" explicitly accounts for the assemblage of land parcels into a contiguous right of way. ATF values for land along a right of way may be multiplied by an "assemblage factor" or "corridor enhancement factor" to reach an appropriate estimate. Alternatively, the corridor itself can be treated as an entity to be valued, and estimation can proceed based on analysis of the income generated or other considerations. Some analyses have determined that corridor values typically exceed ATF appraisals by a factor of two to six.[4] In more recent transactions involving fiber optic corridors, the prices paid exceed the ATF land values by much higher multiples.

The most important legal concept in the analysis of land-based values is "highest and best use." Defined as the "most profitable likely use"[5] at the time of appraisal, this standard of fair market value is frequently applied in eminent domain proceedings. Applying the before-and-after rule, for example, would involve two distinct estimates of highest and best use, one with the easement and one without. Thus if the presence of a pipeline on a property prevents the construction of a home, the pipeline easement could have considerable value. The use under consideration must be physically possible, appropriately supported, and financially feasible for the given parcel.

Whether value realized by the purchaser of a right of way can be included in highest-and-best-use analysis is a matter of debate. In the *Appraisal Journal* (January 1989), George Karvel argues that the high rents arising out of value to the buyer must be ignored in eminent domain appraisals. "Regardless of the benefits to be derived or costs to be avoided, a public utility with the right of eminent domain is responsible only for the diminution in value or loss to the principal corridor occupant."[6] In a response, Charles Seymour agrees that compensation should not include any "special" value to the buyer. But one of the damages incurred by the occupant "is surely the loss of the right to sell to someone else who would pay more than [the buyer] suggests, as indicated by market data."[7] Both authors agree that appraisals for private market transactions should account for values to both the buyer and the seller.

A Willing Buyer and Seller

Private market outcomes reflect mutually beneficial agreements between a willing buyer and seller. One approach to fair market value estimation involves the attempt to replicate the results of free-market bargaining and negotiation. The following court opinion describes this approach as a legal standard for eminent domain proceedings:

> In determining this fair market value, a court must consider what a rational seller, willing but not obliged to sell, would take for the property, and what a rational buyer, willing but not obligated to buy, would pay for the property, and must take into account "[a]ll considerations that might fairly be brought forward and given substantial weight in bargaining between an owner willing to sell and a purchaser desiring to buy."[8]

In right-of-way transactions, the seller will be concerned with the value of alternative uses of the land and the likelihood of finding a better offer. The buyer will be concerned with the income generated and the costs of acquiring some other route. The difference between the seller's alternative value and the buyer's alternative cost represents the cooperative surplus of the potential right-of-way sale. In "Valuing Easements: A Simple Bargaining Framework"[9] authors Joseph Trefzger and Henry Munneke advocate dividing the surplus based on case-by-case considerations.

The cost of acquiring an alternative route, or "build-around cost," has played an increasingly important role in recent fiber-optic transactions. Much of this has to do with the rapid expansion of the market for fiber capacity and the competitive advantage that accrues to those with early access to a fiber network. The cost of delay in acquiring alternative routes is in many cases more significant than any drawbacks of additional construction or technical network constraints. While build-around cost represents an upper bound on the price of a right of way, a large build-around cost increases the buyer's willingness to pay and enhances the bargaining position of the seller.

Income-Based Methods

Numerous assets contribute to the income and value of an enterprise. These include the building in which a company's headquarters are housed, the patents a company owns, and even the intangible asset referred to as "good will." These assets produce value for an enterprise based on the role they play in an integrated business strategy. A corporate headquarters in Manhattan may be extremely valuable to one company or an egregious waste of money for another.

With income-based methods for valuing rights of way, the route used to create a fiber-optic network is viewed as an income-generating asset. Such an asset would be expected to earn a reasonable return. In some cases the owner of a right of way might wish to retain ownership and earn a return in the form of annual payments. An example of this would be the New York State Thruway Authority, which collects a percentage of "user fees" generated by the length of fiber-optic cable installed[10]. In other cases, projected future returns can be added together as an estimate of current market value. An example of this approach will be presented later in this report.

Comparable Transactions

Prices paid in actual market transactions provide direct data on fair market value. This appraisal method depends on the availability of comparable sales data, verification of the data, and the degree of comparability. Proper analysis of comparable sales also requires adjustment for time differences and analysis of historical trends. Market prices fix the higher limit of value in a declining market and the lower limit of value in a static or advancing market.[11] A wide variety of conditions and prices can create difficulties in finding the right comparison. A verifiable set of comparable sales must be viewed as a tool for identifying market trends and a basis for establishing a range of possible appraisal values.

Three important factors used in comparing relevant transactions are worth describing. First is exclusivity. An agreement providing an exclusive right of way is worth more than a nonexclusive sale. Most fiber optic agreements are nonexclusive in nature. Any agreement significantly limiting access to competing fiber-optic companies can be subject to challenge under the Telecommunications Act of 1996. Second is geographic location. Traditionally, a right of way in an urban setting was worth more than a right of way that crosses rural terrain. This difference was based largely on the higher land values that prevail in populated areas. Today, the importance of geographic location is based more on the position of a route in a larger network. For example, a right of way that connects two major centers is especially valuable. Finally, the length of a right of way is significant. Longer right-of-way routes are typically assessed at a lower value per mile. This pricing pattern arises out of certain fixed costs to the seller associated with each transaction, such as the time and expense of the negotiation process. There may also be increased bargaining persistence on the part of the buyer when a larger total sum is involved.

An analysis of comparable transactions has the advantage that values in the marketplace account for much of the information described in previous sections. Market transactions are negotiated by willing buyers and sellers. Agents in the transactions have an incentive to investigate the value of a right-of-way corridor and the price of adjacent land. In a well functioning market, any right-of-way sale represents an implicit accounting of potential future income and a reasonable return.

IV. PUBLIC POLICY CONSIDERATIONS

The valuation methods described in the previous section provide guidance in determining the market value of a right of way. Two additional considerations have bearing on fair market value and are important in a public policy context. These are the value of protecting sanctuary resources and the value of supporting the telecommunications infrastructure.

Protecting Sanctuary Resources

There is an environmental loss associated with allowing cables in sanctuaries. There are direct impacts of installation, such as the digging of a trench for cable burial. There is also an amenity loss associated with the presence of fiber-optic cables on the sanctuary floor, which occurs apart from any direct environmental impacts. This reflects the value of the protected status of a sanctuary, sheltered from encroachment by new economic uses and managed with a bias toward relieving the burdens of human use rather than adding new ones. Trust is placed in decision-makers to conserve and protect these designated areas, even in the face of unforeseeable economic and political demands. If undersea cables could be routed around sanctuaries at a reasonable cost, many people would prefer to keep them out, and this preference has value.

From the standpoint of economic efficiency, the costs associated with crossing a sanctuary should be borne by the company seeking to do so. These include total costs for the granting of permits, cable installation, monitoring, and environmental loss. If the economic benefit of installing a fiber optic cable across a marine sanctuary exceeds the total cost, the cable should be installed. If the cost exceeds the benefit, the cable should not be installed. Only if the relevant environmental costs are reflected in the price of access can government authorities ensure that the company seeking a permit will make the most appropriate decision.

While the monetary value of the relevant environmental loss has not been estimated, it is reasonable to believe such estimation may be unnecessary. Environmental amenity value effectively places a lower bound on the fair market fee. From a valuation perspective, the public would not be a willing seller at a price below this lower bound. From an economic efficiency standpoint, a lower bound on the fee would ensure that correct economic incentives are established. Since, by this line of reasoning, amenity value is not additive with market prices, it need not be explicitly calculated if market comparables are sufficiently high. It is left to the judgment of policymakers to determine whether market prices at a given time appropriately reflect the environmental value of a sanctuary.

Supporting the Telecommunications Infrastructure

There are significant benefits associated with the global expansion of fiber optic networks. Rapid, high-quality voice and data transmission allows companies throughout the economy to improve productivity. Consumers have benefited directly from access to better telecommunications and a wealth of on-line resources. It is an important objective of government to assist in the development of an advanced telecommunications infrastructure where such assistance is warranted, and to ensure that unreasonable obstacles to development are not imposed.

The value to consumers and businesses of a fiber-optic network is reflected in market transactions. A company seeking to expand an undersea cable network estimates the market demand for services it will provide, weighs these against the costs, and decides what and where to build. If benefits of cable networks exist which are not reflected in market prices, then government assistance to cable companies might be warranted. If obstacles are imposed on the expansion of cable networks, and these obstacles do not reflect genuine economic costs, they should be reduced if possible.

It is unlikely that any such benefits or obstacles exist in the context of placing undersea cables in marine sanctuaries. It should be noted that the relevant benefits would apply to placing a cable in a sanctuary as opposed to another route. Non-market benefits associated with cable networks generally, if they exist at all, should not influence the cost of sanctuary access. The need to reduce obstacles to cable expansion may militate against imposing a fair market fee that is too high. While a correct estimate of market value is based on asset valuation theory not economic efficiency, public policy considerations may be viewed as important in setting a fair market fee. This is especially true if there is a range of reasonable market-value estimates.

V. PERMITTING POLICIES AT OTHER FEDERAL AGENCIES

Several agencies of the federal government have authority over extensive public lands. These include the Bureau of Land Management, the Forest Service, the Fish and Wildlife Service, the National Park Service and the Bureau of Indian Affairs. In recent years the issue of permits for fiber-optic cables has come to the attention of all of these agencies. All of them are directed to collect fair market value for their permits under both OMB Circular A-25 and individual agency regulations. The current status of permit fee policies at these agencies is summarized below.

The Bureau of Land Management (BLM) and the Forest Service have been involved in a joint effort to determine the appropriate fair-market fee for fiber-optic permits. Ultimately, the agencies expect to incorporate revised, market-value fees into regulations governing their permitting activities. That effort is currently on hold.

The Bureau of Land Management (BLM) administers 264 million acres, most of it in the western states including Alaska. Public lands in the National Forest system amount to 192 million acres. Together, BLM and the Forest Service issue dozens of right-of-way permits to fiber-optic companies each year. Both agencies currently assess right-of-way fees based on land values using a schedule developed in the 1980s. Those fees are typically paid annually. Converted to a one-time fee in perpetuity, the fees amount to

$100 to $200 per mile. Forest Service and BLM permits include a clause requiring permit recipients to pay revised fair-market fees should an updated policy be established.

The trust lands of the Fish and Wildlife Service consist mainly of the National Wildlife Refuge system, totaling about 90 million acres. Right-of-way permits are issued if a refuge manager determines that the authorized use does not conflict with the management mission of conservation and resource protection. Fair market value is determined at the regional level in the Division of Realty using case-by-case appraisals. There is no system-wide policy regarding fiber-optic permits.

The National Park System comprises 378 areas covering more than 83 million acres in 49 States. Park Service appraisers in the various regional divisions assess fair market value for special-use permits. There is no standardized schedule of fees. Based on analysis of comparable transactions and guided by reports from both the General Accounting Office and the Inspector General urging higher fees, some park authorities have responded to the new fiber-optic market conditions.

The U.S. trust lands administered by the Bureau of Indian Affairs total 56 million acres, most of it consisting of Indian reservations. Indian tribes are free to negotiate right-of-way settlements on reservation territory and to agree to terms as they see fit. However, BIA officials have established rules requiring that right-of-way payments reflect fair market value. A selection of available data indicates that these payments range from $30,000 per mile to well over $100,000 per mile. Additional detail on these transactions is provided in the appendix containing a study by the Center for Applied Research.

VI. ANALYSIS OF FAIR MARKET VALUE

In the sections that follow, information and analysis from a variety of sources is presented regarding the determination of fair market value for a fiber-optic cable special use permit. First, recent price trends are examined, showing the rapid rise during the 1990s in right-of-way fees in the private sector. Next, the incentives of a willing buyer and seller are explored, including the minimum and maximum price of a freely negotiated outcome. In the third section, values are estimated using an income-allocation approach. Finally, several right of way transactions are presented in detail. Each of them was based on a thorough research effort and they serve as reliable indications of important market characteristics. Ultimately, this report will recommend reliance on market comparables as the most appropriate approach to valuation. Much of the information presented below provides context for that recommendation. As noted previously, market conditions are subject to change. A final determination of fair market value should include consideration of the most recent data available, in addition to the analysis presented below.

Market Trends in Fiber Optic Rights Of Way

Right-of-way transactions traditionally involved oil and gas pipelines and cables for telephone and power transmission. The right-of-way buyers were typically government agencies or regulated utilities with the power of eminent domain. Valuation emphasized traditional appraisal techniques, such as across-the-fence values and the before-and-after rule, and compensation reflected measurable losses to the seller.

In 1984 MCI installed the world's first fiber-optic cable, running along the Amtrak right of way between Washington D.C. and New York City. Since then the market for right-of-way access has been transformed, as highly profitable, unregulated firms have responded to the burgeoning demand for fiber-optic capacity. Informed sellers, cognizant of the telecommunication industry's ability and willingness to pay, have negotiated easement values dramatically upward. Loss to the seller was discarded as a standard of value in the private sector, with greater emphasis placed on the value to the buyer and the costs to cable companies of selecting alternative routes.

The current market is still in flux. Negotiated values vary widely as market participants attempt to learn from recent transactions while keeping pace with plans for new capacity expansion. The economic slowdown in 2001 and 2002 has caused a decline in new easement transactions and may have led to lower market right-of-way values. Despite the uncertainties, an increasing price trend was evident throughout the 1990s. A study performed for the National Park Service collected a series of historical right-of-way transactions. For purchases of underground fiber-optic rights of way greater than 5 miles in length, price levels rose from $8,026 per mile in 1987 to $11,880 per mile in 1993 to $100,042 in 1997.[12] Other figures for shorter distances followed a similar trend. Throughout this paper, all figures are converted to per-mile one-time charges for easements in perpetuity unless otherwise noted. Values for shorter time periods can be determined using an appropriate discount rate.

Current right of way values and future price trends are somewhat uncertain. Availability of transactions data has been hindered by the reluctance of the telecommunication industry to reveal their negotiated prices. Current data has been especially scarce due to a decline in activity associated with the economic slowdown. Industry analysis projects a decline in new cable deployment in 2002, with a return to an increasing trend in 2003. Total new deployment worldwide is projected to reach new record highs in 2004.[13] While prices are more volatile than real economic activity, and past price trends may have been unsustainable, it is reasonable to believe that the range of right of way values observed in the 1990s are indicative of future values.

Figure 1 below shows the pattern of rising right-of-way fees for fiber-optic access over the past 15 years. The few data available for the mid-1980s show an average price per mile of about $35,000 in that period. Better data are available for the period 1993 to 1999, when the price trend increased from roughly $60,000 per mile to over $90,000 per mile. The trend line shown reflects an assumption of linear growth. Other possible assumptions about the form of the growth trend, such as an exponential or polynomial pattern, were similar in their statistical fit and reflected a similar upward trend. The most recent transaction shown is dated March 2001, for about $40,000 per mile. It was a class action legal settlement involving the telecommunications company T-Cubed. The lack of additional recent data and the somewhat lower value reflect the current economic climate. Also, NMSP was unable to devote resources to a more thorough investigation of the market as was conducted in earlier stages of its fair market value research.

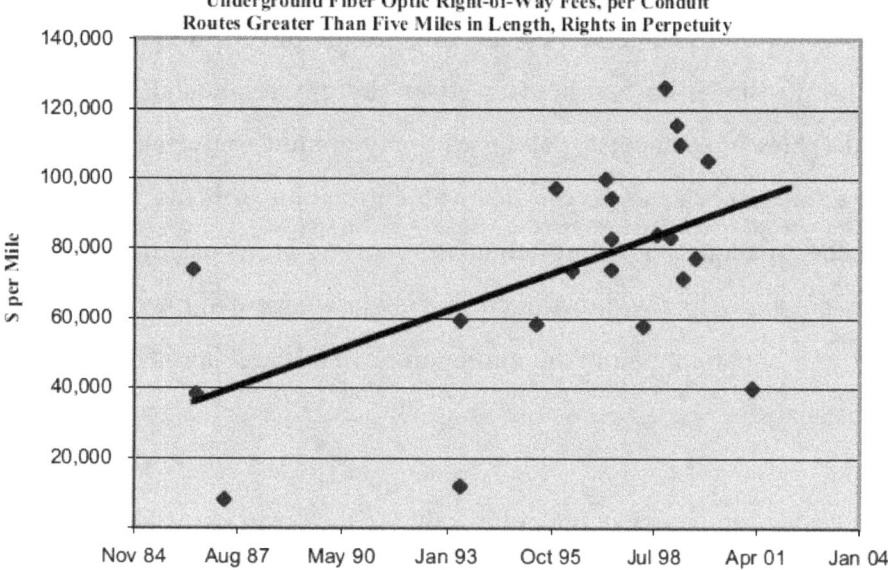

Figure 1
Previous Transactions (Linear Trend)
Underground Fiber Optic Right-of-Way Fees, per Conduit
Routes Greater Than Five Miles in Length, Rights in Perpetuity

Any attempt to systematically analyze right-of-way transactions will be flawed due to the confidential nature of many agreements. Even data on transactions that are not confidential are only sporadically available, with much of it traded informally among appraisers and industry experts. Figure 1 presents all the data able to be obtained at the time of this report, with transactions limited to underground fiber-optic cables and routes at least five miles in length. Fees for shorter routes are excluded because they are comparatively erratic and are often not negotiated on a per-mile basis. Fees for overhead fiber-optic cables were deemed less relevant to a sanctuary special use permit. When several conduits are buried in a single right-of-way, the fee was averaged over the total length of all conduits to arrive at a conservative figure. Any transactions involving solely in-kind payments, such as free fiber-optic capacity, are difficult to value and are therefore excluded. Additional detail for the transactions shown is included later in the report and in the supporting table entitled "Calculation of Selected Right-of-Way Fees," available in the appendices.

The Willing Buyer and Seller Scenario

The range of possible outcomes in a market transaction is limited on the low end by the value to the seller on the high end by the value to the buyer. In the case of a sanctuary permit, value to the seller can be viewed as the environmental loss caused by the intrusion of cables in a sanctuary, along with any administrative and monitoring costs. This is the minimum price of access. The value to the buyer is the "build-around" cost, that is, the cost of acquiring some alternative route. As previously noted, the special-use permit does not apply to any direct environmental damage that may be caused by cable installation. An important part of the minimum price of the seller is therefore beyond the scope of this analysis.

Some conclusions can be drawn regarding value to the buyer. Sanctuaries typically cover large territories and cable companies have a limited number of preferred landing sites for undersea cables. Thus alternative routes of a reasonable cost in the company's view may not be available in some cases. In a free-market bargaining scenario, the negotiated price would therefore be high. However, a specific figure for build-around cost for a sanctuary would vary from project to project and would be difficult to estimate. The business strategies and technological constraints of a particular telecommunications company are unknown to policymakers. The costs of alternative routes involve additional construction, but also include the unknown variables of right-of-way negotiation and cable network reconfiguration. Furthermore, the size and location of sanctuary territory entails market power unlike what is typically observed in private market transactions. For these reasons, the willing-buyer-and-seller approach is not recommended as the most appropriate valuation methodology.

The Income Allocation Approach

Participants in fiber-optic transactions have increasingly taken the view that a right of way is an asset that has value to an enterprise and that income allocation is the key to asset valuation. These income-based transactions take two forms. Many recent agreements stipulate that a percentage of "user fees" for the installed cable must be paid to the right-of-way owner. Under such arrangements the landholder essentially retains ownership of the route and collects periodic payments that represent a reasonable return for use of the asset. Other transactions involve the sale of a right of way, with the selling price based on discounted future cash flows.

NMSP commissioned two analyses of income-based fair market value. Those studies are contained in Appendix One of this report.[14] The studies were completed in May and September of 2000, and no attempt has been made to update the results based on recent data. They are described here for the purpose of illustration, with the caveat that current market conditions might lead to different results.

The income-based analysis by the Center for Applied Research applies industry-wide profitability figures the Global Crossing project that traverses the Olympic Coast sanctuary and is already complete. The full study, contained in the appendices, also addresses a project formerly proposed for the Monterey Bay Sanctuary. Since the permit application for that project has been withdrawn, it is not described here. Two figures are given for fair market value. The first is based on route-miles: that is, net income from fiber-optic operations is allocated based Crossing project, figures are calculated assuming a 25-year lease, a term length common on total miles traversed by a fiber-optic network. The second figure is based on fiber-miles. This means that income is allocated based on the total length of buried fiber in a cable network. The per-fiber value is then multiplied by the number of fibers in a particular cable segment. A fiber-optic cable might include as few as four fibers or may contain 144 or more. The route-miles analysis views a right of way as a land-based commodity, with a market price determined by the typical fiber-optic installation. This view is still common in the marketplace, especially with regard to comparable transactions, where route-miles are the standard unit of comparison. By contrast, the fiber-miles analysis accounts for differences in capacity and reflects recent transactions that charge based on the quantity of buried fiber.

A complete description of the methodology is contained in the Appendix. Generally, data was collected from a group of companies that operate fiber-optic networks. The study emphasizes large, mature companies and does not consider any companies whose profits are negative. Many of these businesses are in the early phases of development, and it is reasonable to assume that their projections of future performance at least match the current performance of mature companies in the same industry.

For the companies chosen, a portion of each company's total income was allocated to its communications business. A portion of that income was allocated to its fiber-optic network. Of the income stream attributed to the network, 50 percent was then allocated to the use of the land and the right-of-way asset. This figure was then divided by either total route-miles or total fiber-miles, and 25 years of annual income was discounted to the present to arrive at the fees shown in Figure 2 below.

Figure 2

	Global Crossing: Olympic Coast Route-Mile Analysis	Global Crossing: Olympic Coast Fiber-Mile Analysis
Total Valuation	$8,426,444	$1,970,826
Miles	65	65
Per-Mile Fee	$129,638	$30,320

The choice to allocate 50 percent of network income to the land rights requires some discussion. First, the contractor who prepared the income study has used similar methodology to value rights of way in the past. These valuations, using the 50-percent figure, have been the basis for successful negotiations with fiber-optics companies. The relevant transactions are listed in a table that accompanies the study. Second, many market transactions using the "reasonable return" approach collect a similar percentage of income. For example, the New York State Thruway Authority collects 50 percent of cable income over the next twenty years on 540 right-of-way miles.[15] In another arrangement involving three miles of tunnels in Chicago, city authorities will collect at least eight percent of the leasing company's gross revenues.[16] That charge could be similar to 50 percent of income, depending on the specifics of the agreement and the size of future cash flows.

The second income-based study estimates right-of-way value using projected revenues from the sale of undersea fiber-optic capacity, or circuits. This approach most closely resembles the type of business analysis a telecommunications company would use in evaluating the decision to install an undersea cable. An analysis using this approach was commissioned by NMSP and appears in Appendix One. The study was undertaken by KMI Corporation, a leading research consulting firm in the fiber-optics industry.

Two important trends were incorporated into the KMI study. First, technology is changing rapidly. The amount of capacity available for a given cable increases dramatically as characteristics of the transmission signal are improved. Second, market conditions are changing. The addition of new cables adds to available capacity and creates downward pressure on prices. Regarding the income a cable generates, increasing cable capacity offsets declining prices.

Using a range of possible assumptions about the technology employed, and relying as before on the allocation of 50 percent of income to the right of way, the KMI study computes two sets of potential right-of-way values. For Atlantic routes, the KMI study computes a range of $12,762 to $76,925 per mile. The average for Atlantic routes is $43,748. For Pacific routes, the range of estimates is $93,927 to $214,576, with an average per-mile fee of $141,733.

Selected Historical Transactions

The transactions described below were selected to illustrate market conditions and trends. The first transaction involves a Nevada Bell right of way on federal lands, and represents an early attempt by a government authority to respond to the changing fiber optics market. The remaining examples are private-sector transactions. They should be viewed as reliable market indicators in that each of them is well documented and based on a thorough negotiating process between informed parties.

Nevada Bell: June 20, 1994

Nevada Bell sought a fiber optic easement running 14,144 feet along U.S. Highway 50A in Lyon County, Nevada. The Bureau of Reclamation (BOR) performed an appraisal based on highest and best use, arguing that a fiber-optic right of way was in fact the most profitable likely use, and that market value was therefore the appropriate standard. At that time, according to the BOR report, research indicated that market prices ranged from $1,000 to $50,000 per mile. A range of $2,000 to $8,000 per mile was determined to include the most representative market transactions. A fee of $1.05 per foot, or $5,544 per mile, was selected for the Nevada Bell easement.

The BOR report noted that government valuation of fiber optic easements up to that time had not responded to the changing market conditions. Traditional across-the-fence or "fee-simple" values were the most common approach. In the private sector, however, prices were being negotiated based on market factors such as the convenience of a particular geographical route, the income stream generated, and proximity to a metropolitan area. The report concluded "supply and demand influences have driven the value of this type of easement to levels way beyond the fee-simple value."[17]

Massachusetts Turnpike Authority: March 31, 1999

The Massachusetts Turnpike Authority, which built and maintains Interstate 90 for the state of Massachusetts, sold access to its 135-mile right of way in an arrangement valued at $50 million.[18] This non-exclusive fiber-optic agreement came on top of a similar agreement only a week earlier. The terms of the $50 million 25-year contract, signed with Level 3 Communications of Boulder, Colorado, included $2 million in up-front payments and annual fees for each fiber-optic conduit installed. The company planned to install up to 20 conduits all at once. Treating each conduit as a separate right of way, the stipulated payments are equivalent to a one-time fee of $112,477 per mile.[19] Treating the conduit together as a single right-of-way purchase could imply a one-time right-of-way fee of well over $1 million per mile.

AT&T Class Action: May 12, 1999

In a closely watched legal settlement, AT&T agreed to pay $45,000 per mile for a perpetual right of way on 80 miles of abandoned railroad track in Indiana.[20] The case was part of a nationwide class action involving fiber optic lines installed along thousands of miles of abandoned and operating railroad tracks. The railroads sold right-of-way access for the lines to AT&T, but the plaintiffs argue that only a portion of the right of way was owned by the railroads in the first place. The remaining ownership stake belonged to thousands of landowners along the railroad routes. These landowners could potentially receive hundreds of millions of dollars in compensation as the remaining portions of the class action suit are litigated.

The settlement figure of $45,000 only pertains to the portion of ownership rights that allegedly did not belong to the railroads. AT&T had already paid at least $11,500 for the estimated one-third that did belong to the railroads. Furthermore, the settlement awards $15,000 per mile in attorney's fees. Based on these considerations, the total value of the fiber optic easement may be significantly greater than $45,000 per mile.[21]

The court determined that the class action settlement was fair and reasonable. "[A]nybody evaluating this settlement needs to recognize that it is the last or at least the latest chapter after several years of vigorous litigation, and then approximately a year of adversarial arm's length negotiation over the terms of the settlement. That is probably the best assurance that a proposed settlement will be fair, reasonable, and adequate to the class."[22]

California State Lands Commission

The state of California issued four permits charging a right-of-way fee for installation of submarine cables. The rights of way relate to submerged lands off the coast of San Luis Obispo County, extending from various points on the shoreline out to the three-mile limit of state jurisdiction. The four routes vary in length from five miles (a single route) to nine miles (including a route into and out of a single landing station). The contract fees are described in terms of acreage, and range from $116,000 to $254,000 per year. With right-of-way width specified at 10 feet, the equivalent fee in linear terms comes to about $280,000 per mile for rights in perpetuity.[23]

This data point was excluded from the analysis of previous transactions presented in the earlier part of this section. If added to that analysis, it would raise the average significantly and point to a higher current trend value. It was excluded for the sake of keeping overland rights of way separate from undersea routes. The Lands Commission transaction is also a relatively short route leading to valuable landing sites, implying a greater-than-average value. As more information becomes available over time, it will become clear whether these recent undersea transactions represent a good estimate of fair market value.

VII. CONCLUSIONS AND RECOMMENDATIONS

The authors of this report recommend the analysis of comparable previous transactions as the appropriate approach to determining fair market value. Most appraisers have rejected land-based, across-the-fence methods as inadequate to address current market conditions in the fiber-optic communications market. While the scenario of the willing buyer and seller emphasizes build-around cost as an upper bound on market value for rights of way, the information required to evaluate build-around cost, particularly for submarine cables, is prohibitive. Income-based analysis also requires substantial information that is not readily available in most cases. Furthermore, expectations about future income are already incorporated into previous market transactions.

The comparable transactions methodology leads to a current recommended range of $40,000 to $100,000 per mile for the fair market value of a sanctuary permit. Valuation on a per-mile basis reflects common practice in the private right-of-way market. The range of values reflects the variability in fees observed over time and from case to case, as presented in Figure 1 of this report. Any figure within that range would be considered appropriate from the standpoint of economic valuation, and it is left to the judgment of the decision makers involved to weigh any relevant policy considerations in making a final determination.

The fair market value of a permit will change over time. The set of comparable transactions used to assess fair market value should be updated to reflect current conditions at the time an assessment is made. As in the current assessment, emphasis should be place on selected transactions that are particularly relevant to the case of a sanctuary permit. For example, long-haul routes, especially submarine cable routes, are important market comparables. Recent transactions and those involving an informed buyer and seller should be emphasized. Also, adjustments in value should be made based on the number of conduits installed in a given right of way, and the term length of the contract. Finally, in a market characterized by rapid change and wide variation in transactions data, average price trends over time are an important indication of fair market value.

[1] "Undersea Fiber Business Thrives on Today's Demand for Global Connectivity." *Lightwave*, September 1999, page 1. (Tab 2)

[2] "Worldwide Optical Fiber and Fiberoptic Cable Markets," content summary for advertising purposes, KMI Corporation, http://www.kmicorp.com/fiberoptics market studies/worldwide optical.htm.

[3] Circular No. A 25 Revised, *Memorandum for Head of Executive Department and Establishments*, July 8, 1993. (Tab 3)

[4] Estimates vary widely. Two good sources are Clifford A. Zoll, "A Logical Approach to Appraising Railroad Right of Ways," *The Appraisal Journal*, October 1998 (Tab 4) and Clifford A. Zoll "Rail Corridor Markets and Sale Factors," *The Appraisal Journal*, October 1991 (Tab 5).

[5] Eaton, J.D. *Real Estate Valuation in Litigation*, 1982, page 62. (Tab 6)

[6] Karvel, George R. "Easements in Railroad Right of Ways," *The Appraisal Journal*, January 1989, page 101. (Tab 7)

[7] Seymour, Charles F. "Letters to the Editor," *The Appraisal Journal*, October 1989, page 595. (Tab 8)

[8] *United States v. 104 Acres*, 666 F.Supp. 1017 (W.D. Mich. 1987). (Tab 9)

[9] Trefzger, Joseph and Henry Munneke. "Valuing Easements: A Simple Bargaining Framework," *Journal of Real Estate Research*, Number 2, 1998. (Tab 10)

[10] "Emerging Trends and Paradigms in Shared Resource Projects," Nossaman, Guthner, Knox & Elliot, LLP and Apogee/Hagler Bailly, 1998. (Tab 11)

[11] Eaton, J.D. *Real Estate Valuation in Litigation*, 1982, page 136.(Tab 12)

[12] See supporting table entitled "Calculation of Selected Right of Way Fees." (Appendix I)

[13] "Worldwide Optical Fiber and Fiberoptic Cable Markets," content summary for advertising purposes, KMI Corporation, http://www.kmicorp.com/fiberoptics market studies/worldwide optical.htm.

[14] "Establishing the Value of Permits for Fiber Optic Installations in National Marine Sanctuaries," The Center for Applied Research, Inc., May 28, 2000; and "Revenue Based Rights of Way Fee Estimates," KMI Corporation, September 2000. (Appendix I)

[15] "Emerging Trends and Paradigms in Shared Resource Projects," Nossaman, Guthner, Knox & Elliot, LLP and Apogee/Hagler Bailly, 1998. (Tab 15)

[16] "High Tech Help City Mine Tunnels," *The Chicago Tribune*, December 3 1985, page 4A. (Tab 16)

[17] Appraisal for 14,144 foot easement to Nevada Bell. Bureau of Reclamation, June 20 1994, page 7. (Tab 17)

[18] "Firm to Pay Pike $50 M for Use of Right of Way," *The Boston Herald*, April 1 1999, page 14. (Tab 18)

[19] The figure from the supporting table entitled "Calculation of Selected Right of Way Fees" is adjusted for inflation. 109,734 x 1.025 = 112,477. (Appendix I)

[20] *Hinshaw v. AT&T Corp.* "Certain Indiana 'Telecommunication Cable' Class Settlement Agreement," Civil Action No. IP99 0549 C T/G, April 1999. (Tab 19)

[21] See supporting table entitled "Calculation of Selected Right of Way Fees." (Appendix I)

[22] *Hinshaw v. AT&T Corp.* Concluding Remarks by the Court, September 17 1999, page 6. (Tab 20)

[23] For the contract entitled "Calendar Item C11" we have 11 acres multiplied by 43,560 square feet per acre to get 479,160 square feet. Divided by the width of 10, we have 47,916 feet, or 9.075 miles, in length. The annual fee per mile is thus $242,075/9.075=$26,675 per year. Divided by 0.095 we get $280,788 per mile in perpetuity. The same calculation for the other three leases produces similar linear fees. (Tab 21)